CATAPULTED

Skillfully Navigating The Process Of Your Journey

By Joe Garcia

"For I know the plans I have for you," declares the LORD, "plans to prosper you and not to harm you, plans to give you hope and a future."
Jeremiah 29:11

Catapulted

Copyright © 2018 Joe Garcia

All rights reserved.

ISBN-13: 978-1981702602

All Scripture quotations, unless otherwise specified, are from the King James Version of the Bible (Copyright © 1977, 1984, Thomas Nelson Inc., Publishers.)

Deeper Life Press

DEDICATION

I would like to dedicate this book to my best friend, my soul mate, my beautiful wife Bella Garcia. It's true that people always say we are inseparable. Being with you, Bella, and living life with you is better than anything I could have ever dreamed of. I love you today more than ever.

Who would have guessed that nearly 30 years ago when I saw you for the first time, walking into English class that we would be here together today? This 16-year-old Catholic boy was not even sure where life was going to take him, but one thing I was sure of was a deep desire down in my heart to serve God.

You had only been in school for a few hours and I can remember that exact moment when I walked up to you to ask you to go out with me, and you said "NO"! Wow, not only did you said no, but you started talking to me about a relationship you had with Jesus and the importance for me to give my life to Him.

I remember telling you that I was a good Catholic boy, and by helping during mass as an altar boy I was sure I knew Jesus. I remember telling you "I know Jesus! I'm third in command...there is Jesus, the priest and then me." Right then and there you told me that I knew about God but didn't "know" Him.

From that moment on every time I tried to go out with you, you wanted to take me to church, so I decided to be your personal chauffeur. When you had a service at your church I would drive you and sit in my car in the church parking lot for two to three hours at a time. I waited for you to finish church hoping that I could go out with you. But, to my surprise, you would still not go out with me alone! Instead, you invited me to go places with all your church friends. That was not the kind of date I was hoping for! Your answer would always be, "Joe, you need to give your life to Jesus; my relationship with Him is way more important than a relationship with any guy."

I could not understand that at all! Weeks went by and I continued to drive you to church and sit in my car in that church parking lot. Until one day I decided to go in and see what really was going on in that church and with that God who you were so devoted to. Not knowing that my life was about to change forever, I went into that Wednesday night prayer meeting. Everyone was praying really loud, and people were even on their knees praying. It wasn't English and it wasn't Portuguese...it was a language I did not understand. I sat in that chapel a little scared and out of place hoping that the meeting would finish really fast. I drove you home and that was the end of my first time inside the church.

But, as the days went on "something" kept pulling me back. I came to understand it was the Holy Spirit, but at the time I wasn't sure what "it" was. When I drove you to church the next Sunday I decided that this time I would go inside with you. People seemed to be so happy, clapping and singing loud songs. The pastor delivered a great message with great passion and towards the end of the meeting he asked if anyone would like to give their lives to God. I don't know what happened to me at that moment, but I jumped up, ran to the altar and gave my life to God. Wow! What a feeling and what a day; I knew everything in my life had changed completely.

I left that place a new person, and I just knew something had happened to me. I couldn't put it into words or even try to explain it! But one thing was true, I had just known about God, but now I really "knew" Him, His love, and His presence in my heart. He was real.

After that we spent countless hours talking about God on the phone and about your relationship with Him. You taught me to pray and you helped me read the Bible and understand what the words really meant. With all of this that was happening to me, I had forgotten all about asking you to go out with me. Now my passion was Jesus. My passion was with the living God. My passion was becoming your passion. Every Sunday after that I found myself at that same altar, giving my life to God. About the fifth Sunday I remember the pastor coming up to me and tapping me on the shoulder, "Joe, you don't need to give your life to Him all over again; He loves you."

I thought, "Wow, I have been forgiven and God loves me!" It was becoming clear to me that I could actually have a relationship with Him. I could talk to Him and He would listen and hear me and He wanted to talk to me too. I was madly in love with a God that I knew of but now was becoming my best friend.

Bella, you didn't just give in or put your relationship with God at risk because of me. No, you took your time because to you God was the most important part of your life. And it was only after you saw the fruit of my commitment to God that you agreed to go out with me.

You were only 17 years old, yet you had such a strong relationship with God that you helped me and catapulted me into being the person I am today. From that time on we dated during our three years of high school, and together we entered this process of building our relationship with God and with each other.

Not only did you teach me how to build a relationship with God but you also said, "Yes" when I asked you to marry me. Our lives had become rooted and grounded in God and He had become the center of our lives. We just knew this was it.

Fast-forward all these years, almost 28 years of marriage, three beautiful children, a couple of businesses, and a Ministry. God has really blessed us. Yes, the process at times has not been the easiest but being together with Jesus in the center of our lives is the most beautiful part of our journey. I can say that today I love you more than ever.

Thank you for not saying "Yes" to me when I wanted you to. Thank you for saying "Yes" to God and for protecting your relationship with Him above everything else. Thank you for being my strength, my cheerleader, my encourager, my helper, my teacher...and thank you for partnering with Him and for being you.

I am so thankful to God for that day when I was in English class and I saw you walk in. Our lives were forever changed that day and I would not alter a single part of the process. Living life with you is a joy! Living life with you is fun! Every day with you is a gift! You are the reason I wrote this book. You are the reason my own journey is complete in Him.

I love you with all my heart and I can't wait to see where God takes us from here.

Today and always,

Joe

#ifitsnotfunwedontwantit

ENDORSEMENTS

Joe and Bella Garcia are contagious with supernatural joy and passion for the things of God! In this book, Joe takes you on a walk with him and shares revelatory truths that will build up and impart greater realms of faith to believe for success to manifest within your own journey in life and ministry. Take hold of these experiential words that are written and receive Divine wisdom and encouragement to continue walking out the course God has laid out for you. Position yourself and get ready to be launched forth into the NEW, into TRANSFORMATION and into His DIVINE WILL!

JOSHUA and JANET MILLS
Prophetic Evangelists, Authors, Songwriter
International Glory Inc.
Palm Springs, CA / London, Ontario, Canada
JoshuaMills.com

Joe and his wife Bella are two of my favourite people! They are dynamic, fun, empowering, motivating and real, especially real. That is what they are like on the platform and off the platform. And that is what you are going to get when you read Joe's newest book *Catapulted*. Not everyone sees the life-changing and transformative principles that the Bible holds for us. Most of us grow by hearing the revelation and insights that others have discovered. That is what this book will do for you. Joe will take you on a journey into being who you are designed by Father God to be!

STEVE LONG
Vice President, Catch the Fire World
Director, Catch the Fire Canada
Senior Leader, Catch the Fire Toronto
Toronto, Ontario, Canada
CatchTheFire.com

Joe Garcia is a true revivalist! After spending even moments with Joe, you realize he is a fun-loving, radical, passionate man after God's own heart. In his book, "Catapulted", Joe gives insights into how we can all be launched into our God-given calling, free of every hindrance. This book gives practical insights, real-life testimonies, and teaching on how to break out of fear, have our minds renewed, embrace the processes of God and walk in the fullness of our destiny. Joe lives with childlike faith, with a spirit of sonship, and with a big heavenly Father. His writing and his life are inspirational for all.

PATRICIA BOOTSMA
Itinerate Speaker, Author
Sr. Associate Pastor, Catch the Fire Toronto
Director, CTF House of Prayer
Leader, Ontario Prophetic Counsel
PatriciaBootsma.com

Joe Garcia is a good friend of mine. I have seen God move through his life and his ministry in powerful ways. He operates in an amazing Seer anointing, often having powerful dreams and visions. This new book that he has written will help you to grow from glory to glory. In Christ, each day is an opportunity to leave the old nature behind and to walk into the new. Joe shares his journey and writes in a way that is both eloquent and simple. You will not be able to put this book down without noticing you are growing spiritually.

DARREN CANNING
Speaker, Author, Prophet
President/Founder, Darren Canning Ministries
Almonte, Ontario, Canada
DarrenCanning.com

Joe Garcia's new book "CATAPULTED" will create a hunger in you for a Presence and a passion for the flame, while challenging you to go deeper. You can overcome anything and Joe's testimony of God's faithfulness will encourage you to never give up! You will be truly impacted beyond measure in reading his latest book "Catapulted". I believe there is a great commission for you in the pages of this book!

TODD BENTLEY
Healing Evangelist, Revivalist, Author, Prophet
Founder, Fresh Fire USA
Pineville, North Carolina, USA
FreshFireUSA.com

Joe Garcia has created a masterpiece! A book like this is timely for this era in Church history, and also for anyone wanting to navigate through "transition" into greater things. This book is a roadmap for today's leader. Joe shares timely wisdom that only the "seasoned" have realized through experience and genuine "process." Read this book and prepare to be catapulted into destiny!

DEREK SCHNEIDER
Speaker, Trainer, Author, Transformation Specialist
President, History Makers Academy
Founder, History Makers Society
DerekSchneider.ca

It is with great joy and honor that I recommend to you my dear friend's book entitled *Catapulted*. Truly, Joe Garcia's inspiring work is a guaranteed source of encouragement for all of those needing a spiritual refreshing. If one would question why certain trials have come or why some of life's battles never seem to let up, this book will offer a welcomed perspective that will fill the reader's heart with hope, joy, and peace! I wholeheartedly recommend the author, as well as his God-inspired work!

JOEL SPINKS
Pastor, TV Host, Author
EMCI-TV Production "Vie de Foi"
President/Founder, Quebec Victory Church, Joël Spinks Ministries, "Le Collège Intégrité"
Granby, Quebec, Canada

JoelSpinks.com

Joe Garcia's book "Catapulted" is plume full of supernatural wisdom from a seasoned veteran of one whose true desire is to see the Kingdom of heaven come. "Catapulted," offers the reader nuggets of truth, backed by solid biblical scriptural references that will draw the reader, if applied to life's real situations, into a true Kingdom authority. This work is a call from heaven to those whose desire it is, like eagles to soar above the fray infused from on high. "Catapulted" will release new weapons for yourself and others, in the ongoing battle set before you as you enter the end of this age.

PETER NASH
Revivalist and Founder of Fresh Oil & Fire Ministries
Sylvan Lake, Alberta, Canada
OilAndFire.ca

It was an absolute delight publishing Joe Garcia's powerful book! The divine wisdom he shares will catapult hungry hearts into God given destiny and purpose! You have a date with destiny, pick up Joe's book and begin a journey of divine proportions. Don't hesitate to buy this book and change a life by giving one away!

STEVE PORTER
Publisher, Revivalist, and Author
President/Founder, Deeper Life Press and Refuge Ministries
Rochester, NY
Findrefuge.tv

TABLE OF CONTENTS

INVITATION

Dear friends,

This is your personal invitation to join me as I reveal the success secrets God has lovingly imparted, instructed, and accomplished through my seeking Him during the challenging processes, continual transitions, and the often, unfamiliar seasons of my journey with Him.

Since a transition is never easy, nor automatic, God has directed, guided and taught me how to say, "YES" in order to partner with His plan to make the transition process peaceful and successful. I want to invite you to discover that in partnering with His plan, He will replace the misinformation, misunderstanding, and misconceptions that have previously held you back and held you captive to fear, religious traditions and old ways of thinking.

My desire is to help you understand how automatic it can become to overcome every unexpected obstacle and push through the unforeseen pressure with complete trust and faith in Him. God has brought me into a place of clear revelation and understanding of what it truly means to skillfully navigate the journey together with Him, with His Heavenly Wisdom and with the excellence of the Holy Spirit's guidance.

I encourage you to press in on your journey with God, partner with His carefully laid plan and discover the beautiful blueprint He made for your life. My prayer for you is that you accept this invitation and that it will catapult you into greater realms, dimensions, and revelations of truth and intimacy with God, the Father, Jesus, the Son and the precious Holy Spirit.

It's more than having a great gift or calling. It's about reaching for God and His infinite Wisdom to navigate each set of circumstances you encounter on your journey. Walking in His integrity and character is what He's preparing you for, and your pure heart after God is what the world is longing for. My prayer is that you receive a new understanding and a clear vision of God's purifying and pruning process. You will see that His tests and His trials are vital, beneficial and necessary for you to reach your destiny, your optimum health, your success and your prosperity.

> *Love and blessings,*
> *Joe Garcia*

FOREWORD

By

Rev. Barry Maracle

Let me start off by introducing you to one of my best friends and colleagues in the ministry, Jose Antonio Pereira Garcia, AKA, Joe Garcia. Don't you just love that name? Yes, you would, unless you were the one sharing your name with one of the biggest drug dealers in the world. This name has made border crossings into the United States very interesting for Joe Garcia. Every time he crossed the border into America they stopped him, searching him and the vehicle. We're talking about machine guns, blacked out rooms, the whole enchilada. This happened every single time!

This is where I come in...

Several years ago Joe asked me to come and preach at a conference in his church, The River Internation-

1

al in Hamilton, Ontario, Canada. As I was arriving at the church God began to show me the Favour that was about to be poured out upon their lives. Joe and Bella were already seeing a measure of Favour, but God began to show me that it was going to go to a whole new level. So, as I took the pulpit I began to prophesy with great boldness how God was about to increase the Garcia's and cause them to grow in great Favour with both God and man. I prophesied that a sign of this would be that the next time Joe and Bella cross the border into the USA, the border patrol agent will just look at their passports and hand them back saying... "Have a nice day". I said, 'I prophesied with boldness', but that was because of the anointing. I began to think later on that was a pretty specific prophecy! It's not like a simple prophecy that a headache will go away! This one was definitely measurable. It was about a month later that Joe called to tell me that what I prophesied had already come to pass! We all were excited and laughed and rejoiced in the goodness of the Lord.

So, what does this have to do with this book? Everything!

If I could sum up Joe Garcia in a few of words it would be that he is a pursuer of God's Presence! Joe and Bella will go to any length to get into the Presence and their lifetime goal is to host His Presence. The reason why I saw Favour on his life is because Joe's greatest passion in life is the manifest presence of God. This is the signature and one of the secrets of Joe's life that will catapult you into your most amazing days!

The book that you have in your hands, "Catapulted" is a great tool to understand the journey we are all on. As you read it you might even think to yourself, "Hey, maybe I'm not crazy and maybe there's more going on then the eye can see!"

Through personal life stories, quotes, and Scriptures this book will encourage you to stay in the process that God is using to launch you into your greater days. In these pages, my close friend Joe, will remind you of much, and motivate you to not give in, not give up and never settle. What you are going through is about to pay your way forward if you just stay the course. Take the direction from Mr. Garcia's revelation and use what seems to be a setback to actually become a setup to propel you further and faster then if you should never have had the privilege had these had these obstacles not come your way. So, as you read this book arise and begin to shine right in the midst of the temporary darkness and allow God to cause you to be that breakthrough for a multiplicity of people.

REV. BARRY CARLETON MARACLE
Evangelist, Author, Prophet at Desert Stream Church
Take Charge Ministries
Barry Maracle Ministries
BarryMaracle.ca

Introduction

Catapulted Through A Caterpillar's Cocoon

Everything that is called 'life' continually and willingly transitions and multiplies in order to renew, increase and become mature, fruitful and mightily used of God.

Genesis 1:28 ~ *"God blessed them and said to them, 'Be fruitful and increase in number; fill the earth and subdue it. Rule over the fish in the sea and the birds in the sky and over every living creature that moves on the ground.'"*

I see this journey in the natural through the processes of nature: from the four phases of the changing of seasons when trees begin to bud and then shed their leaves bare in winter months. I see it in the transformation of the lowly caterpillar into the beautiful, majestic butterfly, and also in the cells that willingly die in order to be replaced with new ones so our organs are continuously rejuvenated.

"There is nothing in a caterpillar that tells you it's going to be a butterfly."
R. Buckminster Fuller

As a child of God you have been born again, are experiencing 'death' to your old life in the first son Adam, and are being raised, resurrected and renewed to a new life in Christ Jesus, the Last Son. Your transition is much like the journey of the leaf on the tree that is born and then dies in its seasons.

If you look upon transition through the eyes of a caterpillar, you simply see the end of yourself. But if you look through the eyes of God you see the end of a thing as a journey and transition into something new and so much more beautiful.

"I delight in the beauty of the butterfly, but rarely admit the changes it has gone through to achieve that beauty."
Maya Angelou

Old beliefs must die and be replaced with new ones if you want to grow and increase. If you don't allow God to exchange and replace your old belief systems you will remain limited, restricted and unresponsive to the leading, and moving of the Spirit of God. And you may even be tempted to blame others for your sudden situations that appear to be delays or detours.

If you stubbornly oppose life's unexpected challenges that change and interrupt your carefully laid plans you can miss the occasions they provide for personal promotion, increase, maturity and growth.

If you abandon these Divine opportunities to your unreleased, old belief systems as 'attacks from the enemy' you will just revive new circumstances that mirror, imitate and reflect the old ones and nothing in your life will ever change. When you are able to understand that these 'pruning moments' are miracle keys from God to bring increase to your life's assignment then you can take the leap of faith towards surrendering, submitting, and willingly fulfilling their purpose.

> *"What the caterpillar calls the end of the world,*
> *the master calls a butterfly."*
> Richard Bach

I have learned that when an unexpected 'caterpillar event' occurs, I have the choice to see it from either the caterpillar's perspective (a limited observation from the earth) or from God's perspective (an unlimited, eternal observation from Heaven).

From God's viewpoint, adversity is not an adversity of the negative kind...but a necessary, wonderful and fruitful opportunity to take notice that it's time to skillfully navigate your journey into a higher path like that of the butterfly.

It's time to CATAPULT!

In order for the navigating of your journey to take place, you must develop a deeper level of trust and faith in God, and His 'unknown to you' plan, so that you travel deeper into it *with eager expectancy.* Don't cower in fear, run from it, or hide from your life's assignment, but cooperate with God's plan as He makes you more and more like His Son, Jesus.

Your Journey Is Navigated
By Cooperation And Alignment...
Not By Struggle.

Commit to seeing your circumstances as God sees them. They are as smooth steppingstones aligned and set straight on His Divine path before you, in order to help, guide and teach you to walk the path of overcoming the little molehills (that appear to be giant mountains).

Proverbs 3:6 ~ *"In all your ways acknowledge Him, and He will make your paths straight."*

He is patiently waiting to share with you His plan, to give you His wisdom, power, protection, peace, and revelation. When you agree to begin walking on the path He has provided, and when you begin to clearly understand each circumstance's Divine purpose, you will joyfully discover a life of supernatural peace, strength, freedom, and magnificent love.

"Just living is not enough," said the butterfly,
"One must have sunshine, freedom and a little flower."
Hans Christian Andersen

Psalm 44:18 ~ *"My heart has not turned back, and my steps have not deviated from Your way."*

At first, it was intimidating and a bit frightening for me to leave the comfort zone of the safe, familiar ground where I, as a former caterpillar, once called 'home', only to enter the dark, lonely 'cocoon' of un-knowingness. But the reward began when I discovered that already built inside me was God's desire and capability (through His process) to teach me how to fly like a butterfly! And this discovery is where we begin to be catapulted...

CHAPTER 1

YOUR PROCESS LEADS TO
YOUR DESTINY

There is a land called 'destiny'...a land full of milk and honey, and unimaginable blessings waiting for you on the other side of what you are going through today. You are not defined by what you are going through. You are not in a prison; you are simply going through a normal, necessary, preparation process.

Where you're going is not determined by when you get there. Your destiny is determined by how you get there. Your knowledge and understanding of each transition, your willingness to submit to the pruning process, how skilled you are at navigating through the hallways of transition, and how fruitful you are becoming in trusting God is what He is teaching you.

It takes instructions, an ear to hear, and wisdom to learn how to habitually and successfully follow navigational devices on your phone, or in your vehicle. And it takes great wisdom and patience to learn how to embrace and navigate the present process as you allow God to lead and guide you on the most exciting journey, ever. Yes, it's much easier to settle for being a lazy, sloppy parasite then it is to allow God to develop faith, character, humility, and faithfulness in you. But God is molding you and working in your life because He has great faith in you and your destiny depends on it.

The things you are facing today are set-ups for what you are about to enter into. This is all you've been asking Him for.

He invited you into His family, asked you to become an overcomer like His Son Jesus, and then He gave you the Holy Spirit, your inheritance as a cherished guide and precious gift. All you have to do is embrace the process: Joseph did, Moses did, David did and Jesus did, just to name a few.

You are either a Captive or a Deliverer.
Deliverers submit to God's process; Captives do not.

Joseph knew God was near him when he experienced uncommon favour as the favourite son of Jacob, and when He had given him the prophetic dreams. But God was also with Joseph in the process of that fulfillment: in the pit when his brothers attacked him with betrayal and rejection, when shackled in the Ishmaelite caravan, when sold into slavery, during humiliating false accusations, and when he was left trapped in prison for years.

At first, all dreams seem impossible,
then improbable, then inevitable.

No matter what you are going through and no matter how long it seems to be lasting, God has not left you alone. He is right there with you. He is working all things together for your good, and He will be with you to the end. God was there all along, working all things together for the good for Joseph, his family and for millions of others. (Romans 8:28)

After 13 years of suffering and struggle, God made Joseph the most influential and powerful person in the world. In the time of great famine Joseph's learning forgiveness, wisdom and planning saved the lives of his entire family, the people of Egypt, and many other nations.

Genesis 39:2 ~ *"The Lord was with Joseph."*

Genesis 50:20 ~ *"As far as you're concerned, you were planning evil against me, but God intended it for good, planning to bring about the present result so that many people would be preserved alive."*

Moses went from the prince of Egypt through the humbling process that catapulted him into being a powerful, obedient servant of God. Moses was raised a child of two races and as a result, he may have wrestled with his identity. Moses had problems speaking, struggled with physical handicaps, character flaws, and limitations imposed on him simply by aging.

You can't overcome what you don't encounter.

He learned to endure the pressure and became a respected and revered political and God-fearing leader, judge, prophet, priest, lawmaker, prince, shepherd, miracle worker and the founder of a nation. He will forever stand out as an example of courage, commitment, cooperation, hope, and faith and who refused to compromise. Moses stood firm in the face of pressure, overcame adversity, and was strengthened in suffering. Moses led God's people against impossible odds and ultimately gave his life that others might enter the Promised Land. Moses endured the process as an imperfect human that went obediently from riches to rags and was redeemed by God to save Israel.

- Moses spent his first 40 years as a prince in Egypt.

- The second 40-years as a fugitive, herding sheep in the desert wilderness was when Moses submitted to God's pruning process that transformed his life.

- His last 40 years was when God catapulted Moses into saving a nation by being one of the greatest leaders of all history.

*What you get by reaching your Promised Land
is not nearly as important as what you have become
by reaching your Promised Land.*

Under unbelievable pressure and navigating the most difficult of conditions, Moses was used by God to give former slaves the direction needed to become a nation of free people whose destiny reformed the entire course of history. He had to persevere and endure the pressure, he had to press forward, and he had to trust God's voice with complete confidence.

God wants you to ENJOY your JOURNEY!

Matthew 4:1 ~ *"Then was Jesus led up of the Spirit into the wilderness to be tempted of the devil."*

You will never be intimidated when you come to the understanding that it was not the devil but the precious Holy Spirit who led Jesus into the wilderness – for a purpose, by purpose, and on purpose.

Remember this...

The successful navigation of your journey through pressure...will produce something powerful.

CHAPTER 2

THERE IS A PROMISE WITH YOUR NAME ON IT

On the other side of...

Setback – there is a Promised Land of satisfaction.
Fear – there is a Promised Land of faith.
Absence – there is a Promised Land of abundance.
Sickness – there is a Promised Land of healing.
Defeat – there is a Promised Land of victory.
Brokenness – there is a Promised Land of wholeness.
Unforgiveness – there is a Promised Land of grace.

On the other side of...

Pressure – is the Promised Land.
Pain – is the Promise of Pleasure.

You might be on a journey today where all you can see with your natural eyes is brokenness and lack surrounding you. The questions in your mind could be, "Can God use me after all this mess? Can God do something with the brokenness? Where do I go? Where do I turn? Who can help me?"

The path is supposed to not only change you but also heal you. In the midst of your brokenness, all you may have left are the empty, broken pieces that you don't even know what to do with. Don't give up because every piece conceived in pain has its own unique place of incredible value. If you don't give in every broken piece will be used to heal someone else's pain. Every broken piece will have your name on it and be a great testimony to the faithfulness of God.

In the midst of what you are facing, on the individual journey God has put you on, remember the magnificent beauty of His Grace.

He will put all the pieces back in place.
He will shine down reflections of love and forgiveness.
He is committed to bringing you to a place of
wholeness and spiritual maturity.

You may pick up a broken piece only to be reminded of the actual price of all you have lost. Another piece might remind you of all you had innocently poured into that experience. You look at another piece and it reminds you of the person, or situation, that may have caused the brokenness, the pain, or the lack.

You may look at another piece and you might see a re-flection of where it appears you are right now: stuck in time, trying to make sense of all the shattered pieces that have now 'marred' your life.

Those pieces were once such a huge part of your life full of hope, promises, goals, dreams, and destiny. They may now seem to be only a mere image of what could have been, just an ancient memory, and a reminder of what you thought was promised. The good news is that every 'broken piece' has its own unique value, a promise and a testimony of God's healing, His miraculous turn-around and supernatural greatness.

The path is designed to change you, purify you and heal you. Whether you know it or not people around you are watching your life, watching how you handle cer-tain situations. God will turn your life into a miraculous testimony and turn everything around for your good if you're not willing to give up.

Are you willing to learn to overcome a little pressure as He produces the miraculous and takes you into your Promised Land?

Are you willing to trust that every broken piece will be miraculously and supernaturally mended and will have your name engraved on it in gold?

*"Many of life's failures are just people who did not
realize how close they were to success
when they gave up."*
Thomas Edison

Romans 8:28 ~ *"And we know that all things work together for good to them that love God, and to them who
are the called according to His* purpose."

Remember this...

A rose is willing to be cut, crushed, and compressed for
its purpose of bringing forth such a unique and magnificent fragrance.

CHAPTER 3

EMBRACE THE PRESSURE
MY STORY

Pressure is a powerful force! Pressure comes to all of us for a purpose, in order to produce and birth something we have never seen before. Pressure is crucial, necessary and essential! Pressure is the answer to your prayer for increase.

You were not born to appreciate pressure.
You were born to need it.

David embraced the pressure, overcame every obstacle and humbled himself before the Lord with true and heartfelt repentance.

1 Samuel 17:50 says, *"So David prevailed over the Philistine with a sling and with a stone, and smote the*

Philistine, and slew him, but there was no sword in the hand of David."

As a child growing up in the Azores Islands of Portugal we didn't have many toys, so we were always trying to invent and create things to entertain ourselves. One of the things I used to love to do was build slingshots.

My Dad had vineyards and he would often ask my brother and me to assist him. We would always be eager to go and help him but I remember as a child I would frequently find myself wandering off into the woods to find just the right branches to make the best slingshots. I collected and brought the branches home to store in a safe place just waiting for that moment when I could build the perfect slingshot.

We lived on the edge of a very small town on the Island called Pico. As a kid, I loved going into town to the shoe repair shop where I would sit for hours and watch the man repair shoes. I loved to hear all the interesting stories that he and his old friends would tell.

While listening to their stories I would take my tree branches and begin to build my slingshots. As he repaired the shoes there would always be leftover pieces of leather. He was always happy to share those discarded leather scraps with me whenever I asked him. And the leather he used was the very finest.

The process was always the same. First, I very carefully used a pocketknife to cut away all the bumps on the branches of wood. The next process was to smooth the wood. Then I would take my two pieces of rubber and attach them to the two tips on the branch. I cut just the right size to build my pouch out of the discarded leather. I carefully cut an opening on each side of the pouch so I could attach the two rubber pieces. And that was the process for making my very own homemade slingshot.

The Azores Islands are volcanic and there are lava rocks everywhere. The lizards used to love to come and bathe in the afternoon sun on top of the black lava rocks. On perfect, sunny days when my dad had no chores for me, I would love to hunt for lizards. I used to go up the road and sit on the walls overlooking the vineyards, quietly waiting for the lizards to come out from the cracks of the rocky lava rock walls. There I was, just a boy with a homemade slingshot, waiting for the right moment.

After finding the perfect pebble I would put it in the pouch of my slingshot and when I saw a lizard laying on the black lava rock I would pull the pouch on that sling-shot with so much strength so the tension could build up and the pebble could be launched to my target...

Wow! It was so much fun. Hours and hours would go by as I sat there with my homemade slingshot hunting for lizards.

Fast forward several years and we found ourselves in a place that we had been in before, facing things in our lives we thought we had conquered before. We recognized we were once again in a place in our lives we thought we had already overcome. It seems that these familiar obstacles and roads we found ourselves on had been roads we had been on before.

Up to that time, we had been building a Real Estate Business and Bella had received several sales awards. We had purchased our first home in the neighbourhood that we had prayed about. By the grace of God, He gave us the house we believed Him for. Our church was going well, people were embracing our vision and moving forward with us. The kids were doing great, we were traveling and ministering, and our personal lives were going great.

But suddenly everything came to a standstill. The sales stopped, and Bella even had some very significant deals stolen from her. A few families from the church left and suddenly we found ourselves in a place on the journey that we had been in before. The stress and pressure of the business and ministry were intensifying and it came to a point that we thought we were going to emotionally break. We carefully examined everything! It appeared that we were going backward and absolutely nothing was moving forward. We were losing ground, the finances were not there and we didn't know what to do, where to turn, or how to fix it.

In the midst of the pressure and the stress, we asked some questions you may have asked...

"Have we done something wrong?"

"Are we in sin and do we need to repent for something?"

"Do we need to sell the house that we had believed God for?"

"Did we step out of God's will?"

"Did God change His mind?"

You have to understand that up to this point we had truckloads of prophetic words on how God was going to increase our lives. We had words on how we were re-digging wells of revival and God was going to do something great with us. And there were many words on how He was going to bless us financially.

We would walk into a room and suddenly people would start prophesying all these great things, and it didn't matter where in the world we were. Every prophetic word would add to and build upon another. It came to a point that I said, *"God, I don't need another prophetic word, I need You!"*

I remember attending a Leaders' Conference at the Catch the Fire Church in Toronto. The week I was there every prophetic word that came to me was how I couldn't compromise and because of that God was going to bless me beyond belief with His abundance.

We were at the end of our ropes spiritually and we were becoming physically drained. We didn't know what to do or say anymore. No one knew what we were going through. Every day we would put a smile on our face. We choose to lift up our heads, minister to those around us, and continue the journey believing that He would bring the breakthrough at any moment. But inside of us, there was a battle going on that we did not understand. We couldn't grasp why God was allowing all of this. He was telling us one thing through the many prophetic words, and yet, on the other hand, we didn't even have enough money to buy milk for the kids.

So, one day we sent a message to our dear friend in California and asked her to pray for us. She sent a message back asking if we would be able to call her right away. So, Bella and I got on the phone and immediately called.

She said, "When I got your message to pray I felt the Lord showing me that what you are going through is not an attack from the enemy. God is taking you through a *process* because where He is taking you, you will need to learn to rely on Him, and on nothing else. He is teaching you what it is to trust Him completely, and no one else."

We were amazed!!! What???? This is not the enemy? We haven't done anything wrong and we are not in sin??? You mean the devil is not messing with us?? You mean that God is in this with us???

The journey was coming into focus and finally becoming clear. We made the decision to finally say, "YES" to God, partner with His plan, and *fully embrace the process*. We knew that this time saying "YES" to God would be new to us, only because we knew it meant we were moving into a deeper level of trust with Him. We knew our journey was shifting onto a foreign path where we had not traveled before. It was like visiting a foreign country that we had not been to before. We knew we would have to learn the language of that land, and learn how to operate in a place we hadn't been before.

It actually became fun to navigate this new territory and see how God was going to provide for each new day. The pressure was lifting and releasing off of us, and we decided to embrace and enjoy the process the Lord was taking us through. Our breakthrough had come in a way we had never expected!

> *Transition doesn't mean you have
> done anything wrong.
> Transition means that God is doing everything right.*

It was at this moment that God reminded me of the process it took to build my slingshots on Pico Island in the Azores. He asked me if I remembered when I was a child and when building the slingshots was such a big part of my life.

I said: "Yes, Lord."

He said: *"Remember how you used to take a little pebble and put it in that slingshot pouch?"*

I said: "Yes, Lord."

He said: *"And do you remember when you used to pull back on that so the tension could build?"*

I said: "Yes, I remember, Lord."

Then He said: *"And you would pull until it felt like it was going to break and then you would let go so that pebble could be launched and catapulted to the target."*

I said: "Yes, I do remember, but what does that have to do with us and what we're going through?"

He said: *"Son, you are the pebble on that pouch on the slingshot. It feels like you are going backward and that you are losing ground, but the tension needs to increase. You are feeling this tension and it feels like you are going to break. But the tension needs to increase so just like that pebble you can be launched into your destiny. Don't abort the pressure, don't abort the tension, don't abort the process because the pressure comes for a purpose and the purpose is to catapult you into your destiny."*

2 Corinthians 4:17 ~ *"Our light affliction, which is but for a moment, is working for us a far more exceeding and eternal weight of glory."*

The word 'Catapult' means to propel or shoot forth, to launch, be hurled at something, propel forth, like being shot out of a canon, and to move forward at great speed.

Maybe you are feeling just like we were...

Maybe it's been a season of great pressure for you.

Maybe the intensity of the pressure feels like it's increasing.

Maybe you feel like you're going to break and you want to give up.

Maybe you think you can't handle it anymore.

Maybe you have been wondering what is going on, what is going wrong and what you could do differently.

The solution is to embrace the pressure and don't abort the process, my friends. The pressure of the process can lead you and propel you forth with great speed straight to your destiny and the great promises you have from God, but only if you don't give up.

Tension from God is not anxiety and it comes for a purpose. You are not alone, He has not abandoned you, and you are right where He wants you to be. He is teaching you to trust Him even though you might not understand. But suddenly, just like me as a young boy, I would release my fingers from that pebble on that pouch and that rock would shoot forward and be catapulted to hit the target!

Hebrews 12:5-6 ~ *"Do not despise the chastening of the Lord, nor be discouraged when you are rebuked by Him; for whom the Lord loves He chastens."*

You are about to be released and launched forth. Yes, the pressure has intensified and you certainly may want to quit, you want to get off that pouch He has you on. But believe me, there is no other way! Embrace it, stay right there and you will soon see where He is taking you!

Another important thing He told us was to be very careful with the condition of our hearts, to love unconditionally and not allow bitterness or offence to enter, or take root. When the real estate sales stopped, clients decided to take their business elsewhere, and some agents even stole Bella's clients that left us with no sales and no clients. The Lord was very clear when He told us to keep our hearts right because we had every opportunity to be hurt and offended.

> *You may have every REASON to be offended,*
> *but in Jesus Christ, you have no*
> *RIGHT to be offended.*

He said it was very important to not allow any offence or bitterness to enter our hearts that could abort the process! We are so glad we listened!

Remember this...

When you learn how to successfully navigate through the seasons...pressure becomes something to get excited about! Pressure produces!

CHAPTER 4

TRUST IS THE MASTER KEY OBEDIENCE USES TO OPEN THE LOCK

Proverbs 3:5-6 ~ *"Trust in the Lord with all thine heart, and lean not unto thine own understanding. In all thy ways acknowledge Him, and He shall direct thy paths."*

Following an instruction is the best place to begin when you want access to the benefits of trusting God. An instruction is something you follow; it is not a suggestion. As disciples, you are encouraged to obey the scriptures and trust Him with all your heart. You are not to look to the right, the left, your senses, or to your mind for help and guidance, but only to God. As you acknowledge God in everything you do, His promise is that He will give you access to and direct you on the path He has prepared for you.

The excitement of obedience...
is finding out later what God had in mind.

Keys are symbols of authority, jurisdiction, power, and control. They keep you either in or out of clearly understanding and navigating the routes you are following. Trust is the master key that obedience to the Word uses to open to you the revelations of understanding and wisdom.

If you do not have a key to a lock, you cannot enter or exit. Keys grant complete access to new realms, heavenly revelations, spaces, and every place that was once hidden to you. Trusting God is your master key that opens wide all the contents and blessings inside those spaces that were once hidden. Jesus has been given the "Keys to the Kingdom" because He completely trusted, followed and obeyed His Father... and He has entrusted those keys to you.

Isaiah 22:22 ~ *"Then I will set the key of the house of David on His shoulder; when He opens no one will shut, when He shuts no one will open."*

Matthew 16:19a ~ *"I will give you the keys of the Kingdom of heaven..."*

Psalm 37:3-5 ~ *"Trust in the Lord, and do good; so shalt thou dwell in the land, and verily thou shalt be fed. Delight thyself also in the Lord; and He shall give thee the desires of thine heart. Commit thy way unto the Lord; trust also in Him and he shall bring it to pass."*

When you trust in the Lord He not only meets your physical needs but also gives you the keys to the desires of your heart as you commit your way to Him and follow Him.

Psalm 22:4, 5 ~ *"Our fathers trusted in Thee: they trusted, and Thou didst deliver them. They cried unto thee, and were delivered: they trusted in Thee, and were not confounded."*

When Old Testament believers trusted in God, they were delivered from all their enemies, as well as their own confusion and fears. Trusting is the key that opens the doors to freedom and deliverance. When you are trusting God a door that doesn't open is probably not your door!

Proverbs 29:25 ~ *"The fear of man brings a snare: but whoso puts his trust in the Lord shall be safe."*

Psalm 56:3, 4 ~ *"What time I am afraid, I will trust in You. In God I will praise His Word, in God I have put my trust; I will not fear what man can do to me."*

The fear of man enslaves and snares you in its trap without faith to stand on. When you are not trusting in God, you are in the trap of fear because you will always be listening and trusting in someone. Trusting in God is the key to your promised safety and freedom in order to move and navigate forward as you follow His instructions.

Psalm 28:7 ~ *"The Lord is my strength and my shield; my heart trusted in Him, and I am helped: therefore my heart greatly rejoices; and with my song will I praise Him."*

God is eager and able to help you, but only when you let Him. He is a gentleman and will rarely move forcefully on your behalf without your words of faith, or your willingness and consent. By trusting in the Lord, you have the keys to open the doors to receiving His supernatural help.

*Complete Trust Is In Surrendering Your
Life To The Lord.*

Psalm 91:2 ~ *"I will say of the Lord, He is my refuge and my fortress: my God, in Him will I trust."*

Trusting in God provides you a refuge, a place of safety. In times of trouble or sorrow, He is there to protect you when you trust Him in faith, without fear.

Isaiah 26:3-4 ~ *"You will keep him in perfect peace whose mind is stayed on You because he trusts in You. Trust ye in the Lord forever, for in the Lord is everlasting strength."*

Trusting only in God brings perfect peace. There is nothing to trust in and no one else in the world who can bring you peace like a river on your journey to your destiny. Your mind is learning how to be fixed, unmovable, and focused on trusting in the Lord.

2 Corinthians 1:8-10 ~ *"For we would not, brethren, have you ignorant of our trouble which came to us in Asia, that we were pressed out of measure, above strength, insomuch that we despaired even of life: but we had the sentence of death in ourselves, that we should not trust in ourselves, but in God which raises the dead: who delivered us from so great a death, and doth deliver: in whom we trust that He will yet deliver us."*

Paul and other believers ran into a lot of trouble in Asia. They could no longer trust in their own ability to save themselves. If they had, they never would have made it. It was only by constantly trusting in God on a daily basis that they were delivered.

2 Corinthians 3:4-5 ~ *"And such trust have we through Christ to God-ward: not that we are sufficient of ourselves to think anything as of ourselves; but our sufficiency is of God."*

Putting God first in your life ensures that all your needs are met. Worrying about finances, your job, or whatever, is unbelief. With unbelief and fear, there is no trust or faith in God and no key to open the door to the supernatural realms He has for you.

> *Trusting in yourself does not make you sufficient.*
> *Trusting in God is the only answer.*

Why can you trust in God? Because He is all light (all sufficient, all knowing, all seeing, all wisdom); you can safely and confidently trust Him.

I John 1:5 ~ *"This then is the message which we have heard of Him, and declare unto you, that God is light, and in Him is no darkness at all."*

Numbers 23:19 ~ *"God is not a man that He should lie; neither the Son of man, that He should repent: has He said, and shall He not do it? Or has He spoken, and shall He not make it good?"*

God cannot and will not do evil. God cannot and will not lie. He is your Father, and you have His gift of the Holy Spirit inside you. Your earthly fathers are human and can accidentally make mistakes without meaning to, but that can never happen with God. You can always trust Him completely.

Proverbs 11:28 ~ *"He that trusts in his riches shall fall: but the righteous shall flourish as a branch."*

Psalm 146:3 ~ *"Put not your trust in princes, nor in the son of man, in whom there is no help."*

Trusting in man will leave you disappointed, disillusioned, dry, parched, famished, and empty. Trusting in the Lord means you will have comfort, no want, and will always bear fruit.

Psalm 118:8 ~ *"It is better to take refuge in the Lord than to trust in man."*

You can see from all these scriptures that you are being taught to trust in God in order to live your life and travel on your journey in the abundant life without stress, worry, or fear. If you trust in man, money, or your own abilities, the end result will be a continual disappointment and even failure. Following His instructions and trusting in the Lord is the only pathway to follow that will lead you straight to victory and straight to your Promised Land of destiny.

Remember this...

Depending on whether you trust in man, in yourself, or in God...that "key" will lock the doors to a successful journey and you will eventually 'fall', or it will grant you a continual all-access pass through the doors that will help you 'flourish'.

CHAPTER 5

YOU HAVE NOT BEEN CALLED TO LIVE IN A BATTLEFIELD

Understand this today...your battle has already been won. You no longer have to fight a defeated foe. Your "battle" is to stay focused! You are invited to believe it, cross the finish line, and wave the victory flag.

2 Chronicles 20:15 ~ *"And he said, Hearken you, all Judah, and you inhabitants of Jerusalem, and you king Jehoshaphat, thus says the Lord unto you, be not afraid nor dismayed by reason of this great multitude; for the battle is not yours, but God's."*

2 Chronicles 20:17 ~ *"You will not need to fight in this battle. Stand firm, hold your position and see the salvation of the Lord on your behalf, O Judah and*

Jerusalem. Do not be afraid and do not be dismayed. Tomorrow, go out against them, and the Lord will be with you."

So many of us live unknowingly in the battlefield, going from battle to battle, and struggle to struggle, in search of the victory, in search of an answer, in search of a breakthrough, in search of anything to relieve the pressure!

1 Corinthians 15:57 ~ *"But thanks be to God, who gives us the victory through our Lord Jesus Christ."*

Romans 8:37-39 ~ *"No, in all these things we are more than conquerors through Him who loved us. For I am sure that neither death nor life, nor angels nor rulers, nor things present nor things to come, nor powers, nor height nor depth, nor anything else in all creation, will be able to separate us from the love of God in Christ Jesus our Lord."*

I'm sure you have heard people say, "Another level – another devil." There is a new level waiting for you and graduation day is upon you, but it doesn't mean you are going into a new battle and it doesn't mean the devil has anything to do with it.

*You don't go from battle to battle.
You go from Glory to Glory!*

2 Chronicles 32:7 ~ *"Be strong, brave and courageous! Don't be afraid and don't panic because of the king of*

Assyria and this huge army that is with him! We have with us one who is stronger than those who are with him."

Too many of God's people have been deceived into thinking they are to live in the battlefield. They have lost their hope and have lost their focus on who they are, and who they belong to. The battlefield is not the place where you belong; you belong in a much higher, safer place.

The battlefield is where the enemy comes to fulfill his defeated earthly assignment...
To kill, steal and destroy!

Through deception the enemy tries to steal your focus and cause you to lose hope as your eyes are taken off the Lord. He tries to kill your faith and bring fear, confusion, and doubt. He tries to destroy your vision and cause you to give in, give up and quit the process. Get your focus back on the Lord and get back up today.

Don't give up – stay in the joy of the Lord. If you let your enemy steal your joy he will go right ahead and take your strength also. For the joy of the Lord is your strength. The battlefield will unleash a spirit of weariness and exhaustion upon you. You definitely don't want to dwell any longer on the battlefield because you already won!

Ephesians 2:6 ~ *"And God raised us up with Christ and seated us with Him in the heavenly realms in Christ Jesus."*

Being seated with Christ in Heavenly places means RULING and REIGNING. It means declaring things that God wants to be established. This is the spiritual, geographical location where you belong, and it's not living in the battlefield. You don't want to find yourself saying things like: "If I could only skip this season." "God, please let me skip this lesson."

If you have been living in the battlefield, the enemy has probably been unrelenting in the attempts to get you down, maybe even trying to destroy your health with anxiety. You can become exhausted there with the negative pressure that doesn't come from God but from being on the battlefield with the enemy. Get out of there as quick as you can.

God's pressure produces the unimaginable.
The enemy's pressure produces disease, doubt, debt,
and destruction.

If you have been living in the battlefield, the enemy has been stealing your strength, your joy, your hope, your focus, your blessings, your health and even your destiny. Recognize that it's the thief who has been at work, not God. This is not your Promised Land! Pack your bags!

While you are on the battlefield feeling overwhelmed and overcome with hopelessness and helplessness you will continue to be robbed of your destiny. You may feel so defeated you want to give up, relinquish the valuable lessons and lose your inheritance. Your Promised Land is just ahead and it's time to cross over! It's time to pack up, move out and move up!

> *"Most of the important things in the world*
> *have been accomplished by people*
> *who have kept on trying when there seemed*
> *no hope at all."*
> Dale Carnegie

You were not called to live on a battlefield! You were called to be seated with Christ in Heavenly places...ruling and reigning with dominion and authority, calling things into order, declaring things so they will be established, and co-creating with Christ.

Remember this...

Since you were not called to blindly navigate through a minefield, it's time to move up to the safety of a higher, heavenly perspective where your vision is clear and you will soar like an eagle.

CHAPTER 6

MOVE ON UP TO HIGHER GROUND

Take your seat with Christ in heavenly places and see yourself living from a peaceful place of victory, not from the old miserable place as a struggling victim fighting a war.

There is a place in the mountains called, *"above the snake line"*. In nature, there is an invisible yet very real and definite line above which you will never find a snake. The early settlers in North America referred to this line as "the snake line". Often, when they were purchasing land, they would ask whether or not the property was above the snake line.

They knew the land on the mountain was more rocky, harder to clear, and not as fertile as the land in the valley. But, they also knew the land in the valley was dangerously infested with rattlesnakes, adders, and copperheads. Many settlers chose to raise their families on the safer, higher ground, above the snake line, rather than take the risk of deadly snakebites.

Just as the Lord has drawn an invisible line in the mountains where the snakes cannot pass, there is a "spiritual snake line" as well. There is a level of living that is higher, a level above the battlefield, above the enemy's snake line that has been prepared for your peace, safety, and protection.

The land above the snake line is a place of spiritual replenishment, spiritual abundance, spiritual safety, spiritual security, spiritual hope and peace, and complete spiritual abundance. Above the snake line is the place you want to be! It's the place you have been called to live in.

Colossians 3:1-3 ~ *"You have been raised to life with Christ, so set your hearts on the things that are in heaven, where Christ sits on His throne at the right side of God. Keep your mind fixed on things there, not on things here on earth. For you have died, and your life is now hidden with Christ in God."*

Ephesians 2:6 ~ *"In our union with Christ Jesus He raised us up with Him to rule with Him in the heavenly world."*

Surround yourself with people who know how to fly like an eagle.

God is molding, shaping and teaching you how to be a majestic eagle, the only bird that flies alone at high altitudes. The eagle is bold and fearless and does not fly with sparrows, other smaller birds, or barnyard chickens bound to the earth, looking down for their daily doses of drama, scratching and pecking the dirt for a living, dependent on the local "flock" and chicken coop for protection. No other bird goes to the height of the eagle! Eagles fly with eagles, never in a flock.

If you're an 'eagle in training' be careful of vultures and raven predators that are cunning, deceptive, manipulative, immature, untaught and unwise who will gladly sabotage your journey. No matter the obstacle, the mature eagle will not move his focus from a prey until he grabs it. You can have a vision like that! Remain focused and determined no matter what it takes or what the obstacle and you will succeed and overcome on your way to your Promised Land.

Eagles love the storm. When dark storm clouds gather the eagle gets excited. The eagle uses the 'wings' of the storm to rise and fly higher. Once it finds the 'wing' of the storm, the eagle stops flapping and uses the pressure of the raging storm to soar on the clouds and glide. This gives the eagle an opportunity to rest its wings. In the meantime, the chickens scatter frantically and run for shelter in the coop, and the other birds hide and cower in the leaves and branches of the trees. You can use the raging, stormy seasons of your life to rise to greater heights that will catapult you even higher.

In the same way as "above the snake line" there is a place called, *"below the frost line"*. When you excavate footings for a foundation you need to dig below the frost line. It is the depth at which the moisture present in the soil is expected to freeze. Once your footings are buried below the frost line the ground will act as a barrier to insulate the soil below the footing from freezing in the winter.

In order to combat the problem of freezing, footings are placed six inches below the frost line. The frost line is the maximum depth where the ground will freeze in the winter. In Minneapolis/St. Paul, Minnesota, footings are required by code to be between 54 and 60 inches deep.

There is a place that the Lord is calling you to live that is "above the snake line" where you are seated with Him in order to rule and reign, create with the Creator, and call things into Divine order.

The place "below the frost line" is where you are hidden in Christ, the deep place where you are to build your foundation. This is where the icy cold, negative elements of this world are not going to affect you.

Choose today to let the Lord show you how to live above the snake line. Choose to be hidden in the secret place and build your foundation below the frost line. Take one day at a time and simply make the changes that are coming into focus so you can soar like an eagle high above the cares of the earth.

> *"He who would learn to fly one day*
> *must first learn to stand and walk and*
> *run and climb and dance;*
> *one cannot fly into flying."*
> Friedrich Nietzsche

Remember this...

Skillfully navigating the process elevates you, enlightens you and empowers you to live victoriously in the high places.

CHAPTER 7

YOUR MIND IS SHIFTING AND CHANGING

The purpose of writing this book, my friends, is that any misinformation and misguided old patterns you may have had will shift into the catapulting acceleration of your destiny! Old mindsets need to shift! Your thinking needs to change, as mine did!

I am sure you have heard people say, "You are what you eat". Well, did you know that you are what you think? Your thoughts impact your mood (your attitude), your emotions (how you treat people), your behavior (your choices), your self-confidence and self-esteem (motivation and drive), and even your body and health.

Proverbs 23:7a ~ *"For as a man thinks within himself, so is he."*

Philippians 4:8 ~ *"Finally, brethren, whatsoever things are true, whatsoever things are honest, whatsoever things are just, whatsoever things are pure, whatsoever things are lovely, whatsoever things are of good report; if there be any virtue, and if there be any praise, think on these things."*

Your mind is a valuable part of you. The Bible describes your mind by using the picture of a ship looking for a harbor. Though you may be unable to keep disease-ridden ships from sailing back and forth on the ocean, you can refuse them docking privileges in the harbor of your mind. You are becoming what you think!

You Are What You Think!

The most important things in life are the thoughts you choose to think. In the course of time, you will become on the outside what you believe on the inside. The enemy and thief of your destiny loves to take advantage of a mind that is ignorant, or one that is pushed around by wayward emotions tossed to and fro from faith to fear and back again.

You're supposed to have the mind of Christ! But a mind that has a victim mentality, thinking they will always lose, that no good thing will ever come to them, is a mind that is capable of giving up every time there is the slightest opposition. Don't be fooled, this is not someone who is "overly sensitive" as you once may have thought. This is a person who has an undisciplined, untaught and untrained mind, not a disciple who is fixed, firm and victorious.

A person with a victim mentality would say something like this: "Please pray for me!! I'm being attacked!!! What am I going to do??? I'm so scared!! I KNEW this was going to happen to me!!!!"

A disciple of Christ who is taught, trained and submitted himself to the Word KNOWS he is victorious. During pressure, he might say to you: "Please stand in agreement with me in my season of testing that I will keep my faith focused on God. Agree with me that I will stand and rest on the unchangeable truth of the Word as I continue to refuse to be moved."

Galatians 5:1 ~ *"It is for freedom that Christ has set us free. Stand firm, then, and do not be encumbered once more by a yoke of slavery."*

Jesus refused to come out of agreement with the Father and the Spirit. He refused to believe a lie, or be deceived by things in the natural. He knew only one thing and that was the Truth! You are not born of the father of lies. You have been set free and born again into the Father of Truth by the blood of Jesus. It's time to shift your mind and your old way of thinking to agree with the Truth.

You don't have to receive and believe
negative thoughts...
not even your own.

2 Corinthians 3:17 ~ *"Now the Lord is the Spirit, and where the Spirit of the Lord is, there is freedom."*

Many Christians have not been taught and trained what it means to be a disciple of Christ, to grow up and take every thought captive and weigh it with the Word of God. A good disciple believes the Word, obeys the Word, follows the Word and thinks right thoughts so right words will proceed from their mouth. A good disciple is becoming mature, strong and responsible for their thoughts.

2 Corinthians 10:5 ~ *"Casting down imaginations, and every high thing that exalts itself against the knowledge of God, and bringing into captivity every thought to the obedience of Christ."*

Romans 12:2 ~ *"Be not conformed to this world: but be ye transformed by the renewing of your mind, that ye may prove what is that good, and acceptable, and perfect, will of God."*

Philippians 2:5 ~ *"Let this mind be in you, which was also in Christ Jesus."*

Many believe the truth, but continue to believe that their circumstances are even more powerful than the truth. Your destiny can only be realized and achieved when you believe God and His Word alone. Circumstances are contrary to the Word of God.

Wherever you are struggling, you are still untaught.
You cannot change your future until you
change your mind.
Dr. Mike Murdock

3 John 2 ~ *"Beloved, I wish above all things that you*
may prosper and be in health, even as your soul pros-
pers."

God wants you to prosper in every way, even your soul
(your mind, your will and your emotions). Think on His
Word, His goodness, His greatness, His truth, His love,
His brilliant light that shines even in your dark times.
Let your soul be filled with the truth and goodness of
God as you shift your mind to the obedience of Christ.

Your Future Is Not Ahead Of You;
It Is Within You!

When you choose to shift your mind and allow your soul
to prosper, everything around you will begin to prosper
and come into alignment. Instead of attracting the enemy's attention with your fears, you will begin to attract
like a magnet the great things God has for you: goodness, mercy, love, favour, surprises, kindness, etc.

You are what you think! You can have what He thinks
right now! What do you have to lose by shifting your
mind and bringing it captive to the obedience of Christ?
Think big, believe big, act big, work big, give big, forgive
big, laugh big, live big, believe the truth and believe the
One who gave you that extraordinary mind of yours.
Your Promised Land is within you, even now.

You are loved – think about His never-ending, unconditional love and what His Word has to say...

You are the head and not the tail.
You are the first and not the last.
You are above and not beneath.
You are precious to Him, His prized possession.
You are already forgiven.
You are free – for it was for the sake of freedom that He set you free.
You are healed.
You are amazing, valuable and gifted by Him.
You have a destiny that is powerful.
You are rich in Heavenly resources.
You are God's connecting point between heaven and earth.
You are a unique carrier of His love, peace, power, protection, and presence.
You are beautiful, victorious and more than a conqueror.

You are what you think! Begin the shift into thinking on these things and let the truth of God fill your mind and your heart.

"He who has the ability to take full possession
of his own mind
may take possession of everything else to which
he is justly entitled."
Andrew Carnegie

When everything begins to shift, it may seem as if there is pressure all around you. The former things are passing away and He is doing a new thing for you and in you. You're being pruned for the purpose of positioning. You are being pruned for a brand new purpose. You're being prepared to birth the new and the once hidden thing He has for you! You are about to SEE the things He has promised you.

Isaiah 43:19 ~ *"Watch for the new thing I am going to do. It is happening already, you can see it now! I will make a road through the wilderness and give you streams of water there."*

Isaiah 48:6 ~ *"You have heard, now see all this; and will you not declare it? I have shown you new things from this time, even hidden things, and you did not know them."*

Don't look for a breakthrough from the same place you were accustomed to before. Your breakthrough is coming from NEW places and they are hidden in Him. To skillfully navigate your process you have to change your mind and believe you are seeing differently to receive the promises.

God is not going to do it the way He did it in the past. The previous seasons do not compare to what is happening now. Get ready to reap a harvest in places that used to be hidden, places where you have not sown before. God is revealing new things as you get quiet and listen to His voice.

Obstacles were meant to be Conquered!

You can only courageously conquer an obstacle when you can see it as a little molehill instead of a giant mountain. To see differently you have to think differently. Be open to receiving a new way of understanding.

Understand with new eyes, new ears, and a new mind today. Ask God to give you a new mindset with new thoughts about your journey, God's pruning process, about His protection, His purposes, His carefully thought out plan, His faithfulness, new thoughts about yourself, new and creative ideas. Thank Him for teaching you new ways to love others, and for giving you a new and clear understanding of the Divine purpose of pressure.

Old beliefs must die and be replaced with new ones if you want to grow. If you don't replace them you remain stunted and lifeless in your being.

"Whether you think you can, or think you can't – you are right."
Henry Ford

Isaiah 42:9 ~ *"Behold, the former things are come to pass, and new things do I declare: before they spring forth I tell you of them."*

Every movement toward the Promised Land brings a new place of pressure. Every time you are about to be promoted, you will experience an obstacle. When graduating from each grade in school you were tested before you went to the next level. So, don't be moved! Simply recognize with new eyes and a new mindset that God's pressure is for the purpose of birthing something new. A brand new season is upon you; do you not see it?

Remember this...

Learning to successfully navigate the pressure includes first learning to trust Him completely and love others unconditionally.

CHAPTER 8

LET PRUNING BE ESSENTIAL TO THE PROCESS

God created you to accomplish the specific purpose of being a transformed representation of Him, and in turn sharing that transformation with others. Despite your humble, carnal beginnings, your marital status, your upbringing, or your age, you are not here by accident. There is a very specific purpose for you. In order to fulfill this purpose, you must grow up through your relationship with Jesus Christ, the Word of God.

You may know believers who have never submitted to God's pruning, who are not maturing, growing, conquering new territory, winning victories, sharing the love of Christ with others, or becoming any closer to God, not progressing or changing from year to year.

They may go to church, but they are in opposition to God's Word and rejecting the purpose of Jesus' sacrifice on the cross.

"Freedom makes a huge requirement of every human being. With freedom comes responsibility. For the person who is unwilling to grow up and carry his own weight, this is a frightening prospect."
Eleanor Roosevelt

Pruning is an agricultural process that involves the purging of certain diseased, damaged, dead, non-productive, or unsound parts of a plant, such as branches, buds or roots. The seasonal purpose in pruning plants can include the removal of dead branches or vines, shaping (by controlling or directing the growth), improving or preserving its health, both harvesting and increasing the crop, or the quality of the flowers and fruit.

To your flesh, John 15 could be a painful chapter; but it shows just how much God loves you. Jesus explains His relationship to you by giving the example of a plant. Jesus is the Vine, God is the Vinedresser, and we are the branches. The vine is the source of life. A branch cannot water itself, feed itself, sustain itself, nor survive on its own. It must draw water, nutrients, and life through the vine. To do this, Jesus is calling you to abide in Him: to draw close to, stay near to, obey, listen to, and continually feed on His Words. You need to see Jesus as your source for every need and continually draw from Him through the reading of the Word, prayer, worship, praise, submitting to His seasons of pruning, keeping your heart free of offence and living a life of obedience to His voice.

John 15:2 ~ *"Every branch in Me that does not bear fruit, He takes away; and every branch that bears fruit, He prunes it so that it may bear more fruit."*

God is the Vinedresser who will repeatedly prune the vine in order for bigger and better fruit to emerge. Any gardener knows that in order to have prettier flowers, or more succulent vegetables and fruits, they must frequently prune a plant so the nourishment is focused on fewer branches. This gives the remaining branches a more powerful boost of energy. If the nourishment had to be spread out over all the other branches, then the tree or plant would produce smaller, less pleasing fruit, or sometimes nothing at all. These branches will eventually shrivel up and/or wither away. You can do the same thing if you pull away from your supply, the Vine.

Hebrews 10:39 ~ *"Now, we do not belong to those who shrink back and are destroyed, but to those who have faith and are saved."*

Is God trying to prune something from your life? Have you ever stopped to abort the process because you didn't understand, or didn't want to be inconvenienced or uncomfortable? Maybe you didn't want to let go of something or someone even after God showed you what He wanted you to do.

God wants to prune everything in your life that is contrary to His purpose of you conforming to His Son, Jesus. This could include unforgiveness, addictions, ungodly relationships, wrong or selfish motives, a job that you depend on for financial increase, sin, hurts and wounds from the past, unfaithfulness, deceitfulness, idolatry, laziness, etc.

1 Corinthians 13:11 ~ *"When I was a child, I spoke as a child, I understood as a child, I thought as a child: but when I became a man, I put away childish things."*

Sometimes people purposefully ignore the responsibility they have in hearing and obeying the Word of God and the voice of the Holy Spirit when He gently nudges them to put away certain things from their lives. Other times, God may force us to put those things away by allowing unexpected 'pruning' or challenging circumstances. That process will always benefit you in the long run. But the good news is it doesn't have to last forever if you cooperate!

I can almost hear someone saying that it's been quite a difficult season! You may have felt the pressure and the intensity of the pruning season as the Comfort Zone and familiarity was being removed from your life. Sometimes the dead and unproductive things in your life may not leave willingly but choose to go kicking and screaming. That's all right because it was time for you to wave goodbye and finally let go! God is saying to you right now..."Your pruning season is over."

There will always be a season for pruning. Just like there can always be a season for planting. There is also a season for watering, budding with new growth, a season of quietness and stillness (winter), and a season of harvesting.

You will go through these different phases of your life as you journey towards your destiny and God's promises. You may think that because you have been in a pruning season you will have to live in it forever and that there is no way out. But, because you trust Him and are letting go of the old unproductive things, God says He's promoting you out of the pruning process and into the harvest season.

Your Pruning Season Is Over!

Just like a beautiful flower or fruit tree you may have been feeling yourself being cut back and you may be wondering...

Could anything come forth out of this mess?

Will my life ever blossom again?

Will I ever see the fruit, the increase and the blessing of the Lord?"

Will I ever see life come forth out of this division, divorce or debt?

Let me just tell you that all of this was being used for a purpose. This was simply the pruning season! God has been setting you up for a great harvest season. Increase is not an accident; it comes by pruning. So, God says it's harvest time; great growth is upon you. The harvest is upon you! Pruning doesn't last forever and the pruning season is over.

God loves you so much that He was willing to help you be pruned so that you would turn to Him, the Vine, to give you what you truly need. God may place someone in your life to share and reveal the truth of His Word to you. Recognize and honor them for you greatly need to hear the truth. God is willing to allow whatever it takes to get your attention because He knows just how desperately you need to partner with Him.

Jeremiah 29:11 ~ *"For I know the thoughts that I think toward you, says the Lord, thoughts of peace and not of evil, to give you a future and a hope."*

You may have undergone extensive pruning in your life, sometimes even to the point of being the only branch left on the vine. This process can sometimes be extremely painful, but there's hope and a great reward as you look to Him, stand firm on your faith and on the Word, and don't give up. Remember that God says this pruning season is over.

You may feel like you're being CUT BACK...
but that does not mean you're being CUT OFF.

God knows what you have need of even before you do. You don't need any dead branches hanging around your life, sapping the strength and the Divine energy out of you. God wants you to produce the very best and beautiful fruit in your life.

A part of the pruning process is in thinking it could come again at any time. That is true, but it will get easier and easier to let go and allow God to prune you. If you think you have let go of every dead branch in your life, God will find another one to prune. He not only wants you to continually produce good fruit but even bigger and better fruit until when people see you they see and hear the love of Jesus.

Do you want to look back over your life and see that nothing changed, that you had no impact on anyone around you, or that you didn't achieve all the things you wanted to? Do you want more out of your life? There is no other way for any of this to occur than for you to allow God to take His great big loving shears and prune the dead branches off and out of your life. Trust Him, your heavenly Father, to do what's best for you, for your children and for your children's children.

Remember this...

You are not being punished in a prison! You are simply navigating through the perfect pruning process!

CHAPTER 9

TIMING AND TESTING

The timing of the Lord comes after the testing of your faith...a valuable part of your journey to the Promised Land.

Joseph's faith was purified, proved, tested and tried, as well as his patience before his dreams could be fulfilled and accomplished. God was beside him on his journey as He purged him and purified him, as silver in a furnace, and cleared him of the charges and slander. God also cleared Joseph's heart of the sting of the painful memories inflicted by his brothers' jealousy. It even appeared that Pharaoh thought of him to be a man in whom the Spirit of God was.

Psalm 105:19 ~ *"Until the time that his word came to pass, the word of the Lord tested him."*

Genesis 39:21 ~ *"But the Lord was with Joseph and extended kindness to him, and gave him favour in the sight of the chief jailer."*

God had a mighty purpose for Joseph to be used in saving a nation. He had a process for Esther to participate in before it was time for her to save a nation. And God has a mighty purpose for you to be conformed to the image of His Son who not only saves nations with truth and justice, but by His anointing and power saves, heals, and delivers God's children from generation to generation.

Psalm 66:10 ~ *"For You have tried us, O God; You have refined us as silver is refined."*

1 Peter 1:7 ~ *"So that the authenticity of your faith, more precious than gold, which perishes even though refined by fire, may result in praise, glory, and honor at the revelation of Jesus Christ."*

> *"What matters most is how well you walk through the fire."*
> Charles Bukowski

Job 23:10 ~ *"But He knows the way I take; When He has tried me, I shall come forth as gold."*

Isaiah 48:10 ~ *"Behold, I have refined you, but not as silver; I have tested you in the furnace of affliction."*

Deuteronomy 13:3 ~ *"You shall not hearken unto the words of that prophet, or that dreamer of dreams: for the Lord your God is testing you, to know whether you love the Lord your God with all your heart and with all your soul."*

The Word is revealing to you that God is working something out in a powerful way; a way that He personalizes just for you, for your success and for your joy. He knows your heart and what is still hidden there. He knows what needs to be removed and He sees the gold that will remain.

The unpolluted, uncontaminated, undiluted, and untainted gold remaining in your heart after the purifying process is a portion of Heaven that is to be revealed on the earth THROUGH YOU. Remember when God was teaching me this, He told us it was so important to keep our hearts free from offence!

2 Timothy 2:21 ~ *"If a man, therefore, purge himself from these, he shall be a vessel unto honor, sanctified, and fit for the master's use, and prepared unto every good work."*

Your tests from God could reveal one of three things:

1. You trusted Him, cooperated with the journey, humbled yourself and have become fit for the Master's use.

2. God's plans were squandered because your personal spotlight and limelight became more valuable to you than the highlight of His Glory.

3. God gave the vision to someone else because you camped out in your revelation thinking you could make your wilderness look like it was really your Promised Land.

2 Peter 1:10 ~ *"Therefore, brethren, be all the more diligent to make certain about His calling and choosing you; for as long as you practice these things, you will never stumble or fall."*

Some will *submit* to the trials, testing, will, and discipline of the King out of pure hearts shining bright with integrity and character.

Some will *rebel* out of pride and fear, and remain satisfied with their big ministries, their gifts, and their callings. But they will eventually be set aside to wait for Heaven.

Matthew 22:14 ~ *"For many are called, but few are chosen."*

Be sure that the light in you is God's brilliant, white light. If you are masquerading as light, cleverly camouflaging and disguising the hidden darkness behind the mask, God will surely shine His light on it. When your heart is purged of hidden agendas and selfish motives, you will begin to reflect the Light of God, looking like and sounding like Him.

Isaiah 42:1 ~ *"Behold, My Servant, whom I uphold; My chosen one in whom My soul delights. I have put My Spirit upon Him; He will bring forth justice to the nations."*

It's your time to be used of God. Even if you think you are unknown on earth you are well known in Heaven. It is an honorable privilege to be used by God but only comes through training, cooperation and understanding of how He lovingly prepares you for His purpose. The dreams God had for His children before the foundation of the earth shall surely come to pass, but your part in that process will only come to it's desired fullness when you cooperate with Him and realize that the timing of His plan is perfect.

> *Your spiritual heart sees, hears, creates,*
> *makes wise decisions...*
> *and speaks for Heaven.*

Psalm 17:3 ~ *"You have tried my heart; You have visited me by night; You have tested me and You find nothing; I have purposed that my mouth will not transgress."*

Psalm 51:10 ~ *"Create in me a pure heart, O God, and renew a steadfast spirit within me."*

Proverbs 4:23 ~ *"Above all else, guard your heart, for everything you do flows from it."*

Psalm 26:2 ~ *"Test me, Lord, and try me, examine my heart and my mind (my motives)."*

It's your heart He is after; nothing else matters. When your heart has been purged and purified you will willingly fulfill His plans and not yours. His dreams will become your dreams. You will be able to prophesy into the future, change atmospheres, hear clearly the direction you are to take, co-create with Him, and begin to walk in His footsteps.

Daniel 2:30 ~ *"And unto me this mystery has been revealed, not for any wisdom that is in me more than in all those living but that I notify the interpretation to the king and that thou might understand the thoughts of thy heart."*

There are people all over the world who have big, well-known ministries that are full of heart issues they have tucked way down deep in the back where they think no one can see them. They may even feel they are too big and too important to the people for God to even take the time to deal with their heart issues. Many do not realize they are a work in progress and they have not arrived.

To look you need your eyes.
To see you need a pure heart.

Nothing is too difficult or even hidden too long that God cannot lovingly purge. Being cooperative with His timing and His testing allows Him to do surgery on your heart so you can see clearly His vision for your life.

Isaiah 30:21 ~ *"And your ears shall hear a word behind you, saying, this is the way, walk you in it, when you turn to the right hand, and when you turn to the left."*

Remember this...

Clear spiritual vision and clear spiritual hearing come through a pure heart that recognizes that the door called "His Timing and His Testing" is through faith and patience.

CHAPTER 10

STEPPING OUT AND STEPPING IN

People can easily fall into a religious pattern and find themselves speaking in an old way, not knowing what they're saying, or what wrong thinking is going on in their minds. Maybe you have heard people say, "I'm just waiting on God."

Could it possibly be that God is WAITING ON YOU to step out of the boat?

2 Corinthians 6:2 in the Amplified Bible says, *"At the acceptable time (the time of grace) I listened to you, and I helped you on the day of salvation."*

> *Behold, NOW is the acceptable time,*
> *Behold, NOW is the day of salvation.*
> *NOW is the time.*

Many of your experiences, successes, failures, accomplishments, and endeavours in life have depended on you. What you think, how you perceive things and how you respond or react can make or break certain circumstances.

Of course, apart from your partnership with God's grace, you can do nothing. But God loves and respects you too much to do everything for you without your willing faith, your surrender, your effort to obey, your agreement, and the understanding of your necessary involvement and cooperation with His plan.

Unbuckle your seatbelt, and get ready to stand up and take the step. The heavens are ready and God is waiting for you to grow up, take your place and be catapulted into your destiny with total confidence in Him.

God is encouraging you to "take dominion over the earth and subdue it beneath your feet". He is calling you to make the courageous journey from the sixth day into His Sabbath rest on the seventh day. Take the step and take His hand for NOW is the time.

Your familiar Comfort Zone was never intended to be a safe haven. If you choose to stay in the boat (your Comfort Zone) you won't need faith and you won't need the Comforter. All of Heaven is on your side. He has commanded you to go. Don't hold back. Don't let fear stop you. Step out; get out of that boat!

The definition of a Comfort Zone is a situation or position in which a person feels secure, safe, comfortable, or in control; the level at which one functions with ease and familiarity without a sense of chance or risk.

A Comfort Zone is intended to prevent and/or remove the pressure you are feeling. But God's pressure is to birth a new and wonderful part of your adventure. Remember, if you don't step out of the Comfort Zone the Comforter can no longer be your constant helper and guide. In other words, the Holy Spirit's hands can become tied.

Did you know that the drug of choice in the Church today is COMFORT? A Comfort Zone is not a birthright or an entitlement for Christians to be careless, disorderly, sloppy, immature or lazy.

The definition of a Comfort Driven Church is....

- They want everything as easy and convenient as possible.

- They want pastors to preach messages that make them feel good.

- They want prophets to tell them all their dreams are coming true this week!

- They want the music the way they've always had it, at the volume that's comfortable.

- They want to sing the songs their great-grandmother sang.

- They want to get rich quick.

- They want to lose 30 pounds in 30 days.

- They want a big church, a TV program, and fame overnight.

- They want their food fast.

- They want handouts instead of hard work.

- They want cheat sheets instead of study guides.

- They want welfare instead of a job.

- They want God's promises without God's processes.

- **They want their destiny at a discount!**

Aren't you thankful that Jesus paid the FULL PRICE for you! You and I are His greatest, most valuable possessions. We are the ones He is infatuated with and is in love with more than anything, for He is LOVE. He didn't go to the enemy and say; "I want to purchase God's children back as cheap, as inexpensive, as easy and as comfortable as possible."

Jesus never negotiated with the enemy when it came to the cost of giving His life (or for anything, for that matter). There is nothing to negotiate about. He knew He was fulfilling God's plan and it had absolutely nothing to do with the enemy. He knew what it had to cost Him.

He never said, "Would it be possible for Me to take just one whip, instead of 39?" "Can I just give one drop of My blood, instead of shedding it all?" "Do I really have to go to the cross?" "Do I have to spend three nights in the grave, or can I just spend three hours?"

Because Jesus was in complete agreement and willingly obedient to the perfect will of His Father He may have said something that sounded like this...

"I will pay the greatest price for them. I will endure the 39 whips. I will endure the pain and empty out every drop of My blood. I will be the last and final Lamb of sacrifice for the world and hang on the cross for them. I will take upon Myself the sins of the whole world, past, present, and future. I will meet the onslaught of demons, fallen angels, and all the power of evil forces in the heavens, and disarm all of them completely because in Me You are reconciling all things to Yourself. I will lay in the grave for three days as I submit and cooperate with the plan You have for Me to reverse the curse on the earth. I will be the first to be born again, raised from the dead, and sit in Heaven with You, ruling, reigning and fully in charge of the universe as Your resurrected Savior Son, forever and ever. I will declare My journey on earth is complete and finished and I will release the Holy Spirit to guide and help our children who believe and declare that Your Kingdom has come as they follow My example of surrender."

Philippians 1:6 ~ *"And I am certain that God, who began the good work within you, will continue His work until it is finally finished on the day when Christ Jesus returns."*

If you think the cross is suffering, distress, misery, punishment, pain, and intimidation; that is just a very small part. But the truth is that the point of the cross is so much more; it is love, freedom, victory, restoration, a glorious new life, resurrection of dreams and hope, physical and emotional healing, a new purpose, new joy, and a destiny!

Jesus endured a part of the cross
so He could get to the point of the cross.

If you understood what the cross really meant, you would run into what seems like the uncomfortable part, the part that feels like pressure. You would never run away from it. If you understood what the cross really meant, you would refuse complacency and comfort.

It's your time to cross over, occupy and receive all that God has planned for you. You can't do it until you step out of the boat and step into faith.

Today's complacency is tomorrow captivity.

Have you always been willing to cooperate with the journey God has prepared for you? Have you always understood how valuable His plan for your life is to someone somewhere, and how important it is for you to be willing? I declare to you that you will never have to go through what Jesus went through. But the great things in life will always cost you something great. It may cost you your Comfort Zone and require your faith and cooperation.

It is not only unwise but also reckless to try to navigate your journey in your own strength. When Jesus returned to His Father in heaven He sent the Holy Spirit to live inside of everyone who believes in Him. And He gave you the victory! As you learn to rely on God's Spirit inside of you to impart the Wisdom and direction needed to navigate your journey, you will be more willing to give Him all the credit, and all the glory. Because of the cross, He truly deserves all the glory! You can no longer publically announce what a great thing you did because it is He who led and helped you, and it was He who provided you with the Comforter, His Spirit of strength, power, and authority.

God gave His Spirit to Moses so he could lead the Israelites as they STEPPED OUT of the slavery in Egypt, providing never-ending food and water. Then He parted the Red Sea so they could cross over on dry ground. He miraculously moved the obstacle that saved them all.

God gave His Spirit to Joshua to lead the Israelites into Canaan. He miraculously stopped the raging water from flowing so the Israelites could cross to the other side of the Jordan River on dry ground, as they STEPPED INTO their Promised Land.

Deuteronomy 34:9 ~ *"And Joshua the son of Nun was full of the spirit of wisdom; for Moses had laid his hands on him: and the children of Israel listened to him, and did as the Lord commanded Moses."*

God gave His Spirit to David when he was appointed King. God filled Elijah with His Spirit so he could speak God's message to His people. God gave His Spirit to John the Baptist so he could make the announcement that the long-awaited Messiah was finally here. His Spirit led Jesus into the wilderness. It is clear that His leaders, workmen, judges, and prophets could not do the work of God without the power of God's Spirit.

Jesus didn't go through the cross and die to give you COMFORT! He died to give you the COMFORTER! The Comforter, the Holy Spirit, is to walk with you, talk with you, and enable you to navigate the journey with power and authority.

You can't have comfort and pressure at the same time, but you can have peace and pressure at the same time.

Luke 9:23 ~ *"And He said to them all, If any man will come after Me, let him deny himself, and take up his cross daily, and follow Me."*

This scripture is talking about you and me, not just a pastor, not just a leader, but every person here on this earth. The scripture says to take up your cross daily and be willing to step out of your Comfort Zone. It's on that cross where the Comforter will meet you and take your hand and connect you with the specific people, places and everything you need to navigate your journey.

The Holy Spirit is your Divine Connector!

Christ in you is the hope of Glory in every part of the process. You are not alone so keep walking forward. As you take each step He will be there to meet you. It is in the place of pressure where He is committed to remaining forever in a deep, personal love relationship with you. He is committed to helping you navigate and finish the journey, the incredible plan for your life that He put into motion before the foundation of the earth.

Gold... is refined and purified in the fire.

Diamonds... are made with intense pressure and heat.

Pearls... are the product of pain.

When the shell of an oyster is penetrated and a foreign matter (sand) slips inside...all the reserves within the tiny, delicate little oyster rush to that place and begin to release healing fluids that normally would have remained hidden and dormant. The irritant is covered, the wound is healed, and the preparation for the birthing of a valuable, beautiful pearl is complete. Like a pearl you are the mark of perseverance, a precious jewel conceived through irritation, born of difficulty, nurtured through change.

Every pearl has a cross!
There can be no pearl without the intensity of
irritation, and pressure.

If you feel like your cross has been a season of heat, pressure, uncertainty, and difficulty just hold on tight because you are in good company! Consider the beautiful jewels such as the graceful butterfly that comes through the lonely darkness of its cocoon and the great heroes of faith in Chapter 11 of Hebrews. The Lord uses those who are willing to trust Him before, during and after the cross, the cutting away, the pruning and the pressure.

You were created for the greatness
that lies just beyond your Comfort Zone.

After Vashti had left the palace Esther endured the purifying and preparation of intense treatments and training to become the submissive, obedient Queen without fear. God's pearl of great price in a life-threatening and dangerous situation as an 'Undercover Agent' was chosen to deliver God's people. Moses boldly led the Israelites from Egypt when he could see nothing but the Red Sea in front of him. Peter was trained to step out of the boat in faith to meet Jesus when He asked him to come to Him on the water. David, the shepherd boy, slew the giant who could have easily killed him. David had nothing more than a sling and a stone, and the valuable lessons and training in God's faithfulness along his journey.

They didn't break easily, have sharp edges, or run away in emotional turmoil and fear of the adverse circumstances and the tremendously uncomfortable obstacles they faced. They overcame the fire of every hardship with confidence and obedient trust in God because they were first willing to be taken through the lessons, the training and the seasons of purifying, pruning and pressure.

"Twenty years from now you will be more disappointed by the things you did not do,
than by the ones you did. So, sail away
from the safe harbor.
Explore. Dream. Discover."
Mark Twain

God isn't going to leave you without help, without a guide, without His power. He is teaching you how to be as fearless as Peter was to step out of the boat, as skilled as David was with his slingshot, and how confident, courageous and strong Moses was when the Red Sea was in front of him.

Joshua 1:9 says, *"Have I not commanded you? Be strong and courageous. Do not be frightened, and do not be dismayed, for the Lord your God is with you wherever you go."*

He is preparing you through the process of His great love so you can mature and be catapulted, shot out of the canon and propelled forth into your unimaginable destiny, your Promised Land, your perfect assignment and your unlimited inheritance from God.

Remember this...

When you take that leap of faith and step out of the boat simply tell your confidence and courage you'll be waiting for them to catch up with you on the other side of the sea of obedience.

CHAPTER 11

THOSE WHO NEVER GAVE UP

The process of navigating the road to success first requires a simple choice. There is no special formula or hidden secret, but just an opportunity to make the choice to submit to God's Wisdom and plan. This decision ultimately determines the direction of your future.

"The most certain way to succeed is always to try just one more time."
Thomas Edison

The people included in this chapter are remembered and celebrated for having the greatest minds, skills, talents, and abilities but the journeys they had to take to get there are frequently forgotten. They were often forced to face the greatest obstacles, hurdles, difficulties, challenges, ridicule from peers and often family, and even the hostility of society. Every one of them reached deep down inside and made a simple decision to KEEP GOING, NOT STOP, NOT QUIT and NEVER GIVE UP.

....

Henry Ford

While Ford is known for his innovative assembly line and American-made cars, he wasn't an instant success. In fact, his early businesses failed and left him broke five times before he founded the successful Ford Motor Company.

R. H. Macy

Most people are familiar with the large department store chain, but Macy didn't always have it easy. He started seven failed businesses before finally hitting it big with his store in New York City.

Soichiro Honda

The billion-dollar business that is Honda began with a series of failures. Mr. Honda was turned down by Toyota Motor Corporation for a job after interviewing for a position as an engineer, leaving him jobless for quite some time. He started making scooters at home, and spurred on by his neighbors, finally started his own business.

Akio Morita

You may not have heard of Akio Morita but you've probably heard of his company, Sony. Sony's first product was a rice cooker that unfortunately sold less than 100 cookers. This first setback didn't stop Morita and his partners as they pushed forward to create the multi-billion dollar Sony Company.

Bill Gates

Gates didn't seem likely for success after dropping out of Harvard and starting a failed first business called Traf-O-Data with Microsoft co-founder Paul Allen. While this early idea didn't work, Gates' later work did, creating the global empire that is Microsoft.

Harland David Sanders

Better known as Kentucky Fried Chicken's Colonel Sanders, he had a hard time selling his chicken at first. In fact, his famous secret chicken recipe was rejected over 1,000 times before a restaurant recognized and accepted it.

Walter Elias Disney

Walt Disney had a rough start. A newspaper editor fired him because "he lacked imagination" and "had no good ideas." Disney started a number of other businesses that ended in bankruptcy and failure. He never gave up, however, and eventually found enormous success and on July 18, 1955, Walt Disney opened Disneyland to the general public. Today the Walt Disney Studios is still one of the largest and best-known studios in cinema. Disney's other three main divisions are Walt Disney Parks and Resorts, Disney Media Networks, and Disney Consumer Products and Interactive Media. Disney also owns and operates the ABC Broadcast TV Network such as Disney Channel, ESPN, A+E Networks, and Freeform; and owns and licenses 14 theme parks around the world. Mickey Mouse has been the primary symbol and mascot since Walt Disney created him in 1928.

Albert Einstein

Einstein's name is usually equivalent to genius, but he did not speak until he was four years old and did not read until he was seven years old. His teachers and parents thought he was slow, anti-social and even mentally handicapped. He was expelled from school and refused entrance to the Zurich Polytechnic School. It might have taken him awhile longer, but he caught on well, in the end, winning the Nobel Prize and changing the face of modern physics.

Sir Isaac Newton

Newton was unquestionably a genius when it came to math, but he had some failings early on. He never did well in school and when put in charge of running the family farm, he failed miserably. An uncle took charge and sent him off to Cambridge where he finally flourished as the scholar we know him as today.

Thomas Edison

In his early years, teachers told Edison he was "too stupid to learn anything." Work wasn't any better, as he was fired from his first two jobs for not being productive enough. Even as an inventor, Edison made 1,000 unsuccessful attempts at inventing the light bulb. All those unsuccessful attempts finally resulted in the design that worked.

Orville and Wilbur Wright

These brothers battled depression and family illness before starting the bicycle shop that would lead them to experiment with flight. After several attempts at creating flying machines, several years of hard work, and tons of failed models, the Wright brothers finally created a plane that could get off the ground and stay there.

Winston Churchill

This Nobel Prize-winning, twice-elected Prime Minister of the UK wasn't always as well thought of as he is today. Churchill struggled in school and failed the sixth grade. After school, he faced many years of political failures. He was defeated in every election for public office until he finally became the Prime Minister at the age of 62.

Abraham Lincoln

While today he is remembered as an American states-man and lawyer who served as the 16th President of the United States, Lincoln's life wasn't so easy. As a youth, he went to war as a captain and returned as a private. Lincoln didn't stop failing there, however. He started numerous failed businesses and was defeated in numerous attempts he made for public office.

Oprah Winfrey

Oprah is one of the most iconic faces on TV as well as one of the richest and most successful women in the world. Oprah faced a hard road to get to that position, however, enduring a rough and often abusive childhood, as well as numerous career setbacks including being fired from her job as a television reporter because she was "unfit for TV".

Fred Astaire

In his first screen test, an MGM casting director noted that Astaire "Can't act. Can't sing. Is slightly bald. Can only dance a little." Astaire went on to become an incredibly successful actor, singer, and dancer and kept that very note in his Beverly Hills home to remind him of where he came from.

Sidney Poitier

After his first audition, the casting director told Poitier, "Why don't you stop wasting people's time and go out and become a dishwasher or something?" Poitier vowed to show him that he could make it, and went on to win an Oscar and became one of the most well regarded actors in the business.

Charlie Chaplin

It's hard to imagine a film without the iconic Charlie Chaplin, but Hollywood studio chiefs initially rejected his act because they felt it was a little too nonsensical and too ridiculous to ever sell.

Lucille Ball

Before starring in "I Love Lucy", Lucille Ball was viewed as a failed actress and a B movie star. Even her drama instructors didn't feel she could make it, telling her to try another profession. She wanted to prove them all wrong, and she did. During her career, Lucy had thirteen Emmy nominations and four wins, also earning the Lifetime Achievement Award from the Kennedy Center Honors.

Harrison Ford

After his first film top movie executives told Ford that he simply didn't have what it takes to go on to be a star. Now with numerous successes and iconic portrayals of characters like Han Solo and Indiana Jones, and a career that stretches decades, Ford proudly shows that he has what it takes.

Marilyn Monroe

While Monroe's star burned out early, she did have a period of great success in her life. Despite a very rough upbringing and being told by modeling agents that she should consider being a secretary, Monroe became a pin-up model and actress that still is loved and admired by people today.

Vincent Van Gogh

During his lifetime, Van Gogh sold only one painting, and this was to a friend and only for a very small amount of money. While Van Gogh was never a success during his life, he plugged on with painting, sometimes starving to complete his over 800 known works. Today, they bring in hundreds of millions of dollars.

Theodor Seuss Geisel

Today nearly every child has read The Cat in the Hat and Green Eggs and Ham. Yet, 27 different publishers rejected Dr. Seuss's first book To Think That I Saw It on Mulberry Street.

Charles Schultz

Schultz's Peanuts comic strip has had enduring fame, yet this cartoonist had every cartoon he submitted rejected by his high school yearbook staff. Even after high school, Schultz didn't have it easy, applying and being rejected for a position working with Walt Disney.

Steven Spielberg

While today Spielberg's name is known for a big budget, he was rejected from the University of Southern California School of Theater, Film, and Television three times. He eventually attended school at another location, only to drop out to become a director before finishing. Thirty-five years after starting his degree, Spielberg returned to school in 2002 to finally complete his work and earn his BA.

Monet

Today Monet's artwork sells for millions of dollars and hangs in some of the most prestigious places in the world. During his life, he was mocked, ridiculed, scorned and rejected by the artistic elite, the Paris Salon. Monet stayed true to his impressionist style, which caught on and in many ways was a starting point for some major revolutions to art that ushered in the modern-day era.

Louisa May Alcott

Most people are familiar with Alcott's most famous work, Little Women. Yet, Alcott faced a battle to get her work out there and was encouraged to find work as a servant by her family to make ends meet. It was her letters back home during her experience as a nurse in the Civil War that gave her the first big break she needed.

Wolfgang Amadeus Mozart

Mozart began composing at the age of five, writing over 600 pieces of music that today are praised as some of the best ever created. Yet, during his lifetime Mozart didn't have such an easy time, and was often restless, leading to his discharge from a position as a court musician in Salzburg. He struggled to keep the provision of the nobility and died with very little to his name.

Elvis Presley

As one of the best-selling artists of all time Elvis is still a household name even many years after his death. In 1954, when Elvis was still a nobody, Jimmy Denny, the manager of the Grand Ole Opry, fired Elvis after just one performance telling him, "You ain't going nowhere, son. You ought to go back to driving a truck."

The Beatles

Few people can deny the power of this famous English group, still popular with listeners of all ages around the world today. Yet, when they were just starting out a record company told them, "We don't like your sound, and guitar music is on the way out." These were two statements the rest of the world opposed.

Ludwig van Beethoven

In his younger years, Beethoven was incredibly awkward on the violin and was often so busy working on his own compositions that he neglected to practice. Despite his love of composing, his teachers felt he was hopeless and would never succeed with the violin, or in composing. Beethoven did not give up, kept plugging along, and composed some of the best-loved symphonies of all time. Five of the symphonies were composed while he was completely deaf.

Michael Jordan

The man often acclaimed as the best basketball player of all time was actually cut from his high school basketball team. Jordan never let setbacks stop him from playing the game he loved. He said, "I have missed more than 9,000 shots in my career. I have lost almost 300 games. On 26 occasions I was entrusted to take the game-winning shot, and missed. I have failed over and over and over again in my life. And that is why I succeed."

Babe Ruth

Babe Ruth is remembered for his home run record of 714 during his career. But along with all those home runs came 1,330 strikeouts as well. In fact, for decades he actually held the record for strikeouts. When asked about this he simply said, "Every strike brings me closer to the next home run."

Tom Landry

As coach of the Dallas Cowboys, Landry brought the team two Super Bowl victories, five NFC Championship victories and holds the record for the most career wins. He also has the great distinction of having one of the worst first seasons on record in winning no games and winning five or fewer over the next four seasons.

....

Successful people believe in taking personal responsibility for their failures and their futures. Their disciplined mindsets cause them to choose to set higher standards and to do whatever it takes to achieve their goals. They have been trained to recognize and respond positively to setbacks, negative people, criticism, and unusual circumstances and challenging events that take place in their lives.

"It is good to have an end to journey toward,
but it is the journey that matters in the end."
Ernest Hemmingway

These successful overcomers faced what seemed to be tremendous odds and challenging impossibilities. Their perseverance is meant to be an encouragement for you the next time you feel like quitting, giving up, throwing in the towel, blaming others, or settling for less than the journey God has given you.

The empowering advantage you have is your partnership with God, the victory Jesus won for you, and the Holy Spirit who walks alongside you. If you do not give in but submit to the pressure, you can also begin to navigate forward with faith, determination, motivation, optimism, and perseverance even in the midst of tremendous difficulties and extreme hardships. If you push forward, trusting God, you WILL succeed and can be used in ways you would never imagine.

Remember this...

Thank you for taking this journey with me! Friends, if we do not give in we're on the brink of catapulting into our miracles!

In Conclusion

The Author and Finisher of your life's journey has already written the book, or scroll, about your story. As you learn not to give in to the temptation of listening to the static, foggy, interference and influence of well-meaning people who would love to try to "help" you make sense of everything, or explain to you the next chapter of your book called "your life", your destiny will then begin to unfold.

God never called you to make sense of His instructions, follow the crowd, follow your heart, or be led by an offence. He said to simply learn to hear with your spirit so you can follow Him. When you're feeling confused and things around you feel chaotic, get alone when you can and remove all the voices. There's only one voice that knows where you're going.

You know now that your journey is unique and doesn't belong to anyone else. If your heart is wounded or broken, it can deceive you into thinking you know the way, or you know what's best. But God said He has a master plan for your life and that is to be whole, healed, prosperous, generous, loving, and kind...as you learn walk upright before Him. He has a destiny with your name on it and will show you the way if you dare to say, "YES" and follow Him.

Let me conclude with this...

There are two types of fear-filled Christians: those who refuse to ROCK THE BOAT, and those who refuse to GET OUT OF THE BOAT. I don't know about you, but I want to be an 'on fire' follower of Christ who is full of faith, not fear, and who is no longer afraid to do what God has called me to do, say what He's called me to say, and go where He's called me to go.

If you follow the crowd, be careful...you might get lost in it.

- In the days of Noah, **the crowd** perished and only eight actually survived.

- After the flood, **the crowd** wanted to build a city and a tower. They didn't want to follow God's instructions and fill the whole earth.

- In the days of Abraham, **the crowd** wanted to worship idols.

- In the days of Moses, **the crowd** worshipped a golden calf.

- In the days of Joshua and Caleb, **the majority** of the spies were terrified to conquer the land.

- In the wilderness, **the majority** of Israelites died.

- In the days of Samuel, **the majority** of Israelites wanted a king so they could be like other nations.

- In the days of King Saul, the **entire Israelite army** was afraid of Goliath, except for the one young man who confidently dared to be victorious as he let go of Saul's armor.

- In the days of Elijah, there were **450 prophets of Baal** and only one true prophet.

- In the days of Micah, there were **400 false prophets** and only one true prophet.

- In the days of Daniel, **the crowd** bowed down to the giant golden statue of King Nebuchadnezzar; only three refused.

- Jesus said **the crowd** is headed for hell and the minority is headed for the narrow road to heaven.

- It was **the crowd** that yelled: "Crucify Him!"

God and you are a Majority!

Exodus 23:2 ~ *"You must not follow a crowd in doing evil things; in a lawsuit, you must not offer testimony that agrees with a crowd so as to pervert justice."*

"A man who wants to lead the orchestra must turn his back on the crowd."
Max Lucado

God, the One who created you, knows intimately and unquestionably what's best for you and each of His children. He wants you to live joyful, prosperous, abundant lives. He gave each person in the Old Testament the same choice He is giving you. He told them to "choose life" by obeying His laws but many often rejected His counsel. The result was immense suffering and heartache. They preferred to follow the crowd and the surrounding nations that lived by their own man-made rules.

Remember God never called you to make sense of His instructions, follow the crowd, follow your heart, or be led by an offence. He said to simply learn to hear clearly and correctly so you could follow Him.

Genesis 19:26 ~ *"But Lot's wife looked back longingly and was turned into a pillar of salt."*

The visiting angels urged Lot to get his family and escape Sodom to avoid being caught in the impending disaster and destruction of the city of wickedness. The warning was an instruction or command, not a suggestion. The angels said, *"Flee for your life! Do not look behind you, nor stop anywhere in the Plain; flee to the hills, lest you be swept away."*

Already accustomed to rebellion as a result of the broken and bitter condition of her heathen heart, Lot's wife rejected the warning because she had first refused to overcome the sin of Sodom that she had been accustomed to living in. She desired to go back to the memory held captive in her heart where all her friends, the neighboring Sodomites, knew and accepted her. She longed to return to the Comfort Zone and the worldly attention she was so familiar with. So she looked back longingly and turned into a hard-hearted pillar of salt to stand right there in her sinful heart forever.

Hebrews 10:39 ~ *"We don't belong with those who turn back and are destroyed. Instead, we belong with those who have faith and are saved."*

> *Your heart only tells you what you want...*
> *Not where you should go.*

You may be standing at a spiritual crossroads. You can choose to remain right there in your Comfort Zone following the crowd, or turning back to ignore what you are learning along the journey. But if you do, you are refusing to be true to your identity. Most importantly, you wouldn't be true to your Maker and King who wants to navigate you forward, not watch you continue to go backward.

Deuteronomy 30:19 ~ *"I call heaven and earth to record this day against you, that I have set before you life and death, blessing and cursing: therefore choose life, that both you and your seed may live..."*

Following the crowd isn't an option when you are navigating to your destiny. Instead, you have been given a choice to follow and obey Jesus Christ with all your heart, soul and mind. Following Him will set you free from the crowd of wrong people and the wrong directions that may be enticing you.

Luke 10:27 ~ *"And he answering said, you shall love the Lord your God with all your heart, and with all your soul, and with all your strength, and with all your mind; and your neighbor as yourself."*

Jesus said that those who desire eternal life must *"enter by the narrow gate; for wide is the gate and broad is the way that leads to destruction, and there are many who go in by it."* ~ Matthew 7:13

Matthew 12:37 ~ *"For by your words you shall be justified, and by your words you shall be condemned."*

What you are pouring out to others you will receive back as a harvest in your own life. When you pour out life it will return back to you in every area of your journey. When you pour out death (bad news, gossip, negativity, worry, despair, etc.) you will reap delays, destruction and doubt. When your journey takes a wrong turn it is often difficult to pour out the good news from Heaven to the hurting world. This is your gentle wake up call to get back on track. Begin navigating with the Lord so you can be a mail carrier from God, delivering love letters to the world. This is when the catapulting of your destiny will be seen!

*You are either a "Peace Taker", a "Peace Faker"...
or a real "PEACEMAKER".*

You can change the world by changing the atmosphere in your home, your neighborhood, your workplace or school when your heart is pure and you are becoming a true peacemaker. Correctly navigating your journey makes you a confident, peaceful, sweet-smelling love letter to the world and an atmosphere changer!!

Ephesians 5:15-16 ~ *"Look carefully then how you walk, not as unwise but as wise, making the best use of the time because the days are evil."*

Ezekiel 12:28 ~ *"Therefore say unto them, 'Thus says the Lord God; there shall none of My words be delayed anymore, but the word which I have spoken shall be done, says the Lord God.'"*

If you have been waiting and waiting, and seeing no sign of a promised destiny in your future, you may have been needing a simple adjustment that I pray you have found in this book. Let there be no more delays!

Let's pray together in agreement and expect a supernatural, miraculous intervention to the catapulting in the direction of your destiny right now!

MEET THE AUTHOR

Joe Garcia is the lead pastor of The River International Church, an apostolic center located in West Hamilton, Ontario, Canada. You are invited to worship with Joe and Bella Garcia every Sunday at 10:00 AM (EST), or watch the live services online on The River International Church Facebook page.

The River International Church

1221 Wilson Street East, Hamilton (Ancaster), ON Canada L8S 4K6

TheRiverInYou.com

Joe and Bella have been happily married for 28 years and have three children: Andrew, Joel and Rachel. Together they are business owners, revivalists and lead pastors. They have ministered in many nations of the world, including Mozambique, Brazil, Trinidad and Tobago, the USA, Portugal,

Bulgaria and Sri Lanka. Their purpose is to passionately and intentionally pursue the Presence of God, equip the saints, and rise up leaders and world changers. They move in the prophetic, and carry a breaker anointing with a contagious spirit of revival.

Joe and Bella Garcia are working on many book projects including a book for children. Their newest release is a beautiful 31-day devotional, "Igniting Your Day", available on Amazon and Kindle. As you arise and shine, read these daily chapters, and quote these declarations you will begin to experience an igniting and an infusing of the power of God's Word in your life! (A Deeper Life Press publication)

Dear Reader,

If your life was touched while reading *Catapulted, please* let us know! We would love to celebrate with you! Please visit our websites, www.glorycarriwrsinternational.com and www.theriverinyou.com

Spreading Glory Fires from **the River** to **the Ends of the Earth,**

Pastors Joe and Bella Garcia

info@glorycarriersinternational.com

"Igniting Your Day"

31 Days of Declarations To Ignite the Power Of God's Word In Your Life

Joe & Bella Garcia

"Available on Amazon and Kindle or Email us info@glorycarriersinternational.com"

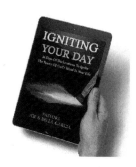

Contact Joe Garcia on

Facebook: Joe Garcia , Bella Garcia

Instagram: pjgarcia & bellag777

Twitter: @pjgarcia7 & bgarcia777

"A presence-driven publisher making your book dream come true!"

www.deeperlifepress.com

www.findrefuge.tv

88550627R00074

Made in the USA
Columbia, SC
06 February 2018